# THE WORLD, THE WORLDLESS

# THE WORLD, THE WORLDLESS

## BY WILLIAM BRONK

NEW DIRECTIONS — SAN FRANCISCO REVIEW

Copyright © 1949, 1955, 1964 by William Bronk.
Library of Congress Card Catalogue Number: 64-16822
Some of the poems in this book first appeared in
the following magazines, to which grateful
acknowledgment is made: *Audit, Black Mountain
Review, Origin* and *Poetry.*
The poem, "March, Upstate" appeared originally
in *The New Yorker.*

This book is a joint publication of New Directions
(James Laughlin) and San Francisco Review
(June Oppen Degnan).

Manufactured in the United States of America.
Published simultaneously in Canada
by McClelland & Stewart, Ltd.
New Directions Books are published by
James Laughlin at Norfolk, Connecticut.
New York office: 333 Sixth Avenue (14).

# CONTENTS

# THE WORLD, THE WORLDLESS

# THE TRUTH AS KNOWN

Isn't it true though, we could ask
—who?— almost anybody, what's
it all about? Yet, asking, not
wait for an answer, or getting one, part
of one, suspect it, scoff, know it was false.
It is —strangely— as though we already knew.
It is as though we agreed, all agreed,
never to say it, to lie about it, speak
anything but the truth, knowing what we know.

# BLUE SPRUCES IN PAIRS, A BIRD BATH BETWEEN

Seen by starlight from the window, fat
blue spruces patch the lawn with darker dark.

Arranged in pairs. People no longer plant
these trees in pairs, with bird baths set between.

Fashions in ornamental planting change.
Houses and yards lose style in twenty years.

Seen by starlight. The universal stars.
Something here is certainly laughably wrong.

Ideas are always wrong. Their separateness
causes a threat to neuter each other out

and leave us without a world as it does here:
heavens and styles collide meaninglessly.

The unsubmissive mind has freedom to be
nothing, worldless—not to exist at all.

Because the various world we sense is not
ever apprehended as one, or formed as one,

ideas are always wrong, always unfixed,
and often their power to make the world real is lost.

Huge factors stand ready to leap in
to alter or destroy a world we defend alone.

# THE ANNIHILATION OF MATTER

The light at least was not to be dismissed:
a hunked-up moon rode a starred sky.
Those objects—what were those objects? Some trivial trees.
Something. Never mind. It was the light
that mattered, as earlier—that afternoon—
the wash of sun crossing the same place;
but it was not the same in a different light.

Would it be otherwise in a real world?
Who could answer? Here, it was always the light
that mattered, and only the light. Once, it had seemed
the objects mattered: the light was to see them by.
Examined, they yielded nothing, nothing real.
They were for seeing the light in various ways.
They gathered it, released it, held it in.
In them, the light revealed itself, took shape.
Objects are nothing. There is only the light, the light!

# IN NAVAHO COUNTRY

To live in a hogan under a hovering sky
is to live in a universe hogan-shaped,
or having hogans in it to give it shape,
earth-covered hovels, holes having a wall
to heave the back of the heart against, or hide
the head, to black the heavens overhead,
a block and a shapening in the windy vast.
This could be said of other houses too.

How it is possible for this to be so
is that the universe as known-unknown
has no discernible shape and not much
in it. We give it the limits and shape we need
it to have. What we want is a *here* with meaning, more
than a vague void moving with weightless balls
or the distant view of a glitter of gritty dust.
We housel the universe to have it here.

We do wrong: using houses or whole
blocks of houses, or other devious
enclosed volumes, ingenious inventions of space
to have us here, has limits. We deceive
ourselves, but not for long. We only avoid
the empty vastness, leaving it there unfilled,
unknown, unlimited. Where is *here*
when nowhere in a place of no discernible shape?

## METONYMY AS AN APPROACH
## TO A REAL WORLD

Whether what we sense of this world
is the what of this world only, or the what
of which of several possible worlds
—which what?—something of what we sense
may be true, may be the world, what it is, what we sense.
For the rest, a truce is possible, the tolerance
of travelers, eating foreign foods, trying words
that twist the tongue, to feel that time and place,
not thinking that this is the real world.

Conceded, that all the clocks tell local time;
conceded, that "here" is anywhere we bound
and fill a space; conceded, we make a world:
is something caught there, contained there,
something real, something which we can sense?
Once in a city blocked and filled, I saw
the light lie in the deep chasm of a street,
palpable and blue, as though it had drifted in
from say, the sea, a purity of space.

# THE BELIEF IN THE SELF ABANDONED

Belief goes in time, belief in the self
included. What was it I was, or thought I would be?
Who could remember? Something of fruit, of trees,
of things that show their form from the start and grow
larger, fuller, riper, in the same form.
More of that form. That was wrong. For me
it was wrong. No matter. There are changes.
        Forms are destroyed.

I am the stripped house, paint-peeled,
dewindowed. The airs blow through. What comes comes.
Snow in winter. I am open. It would be wrong
to speak of growing. Fruit and trees no more.
And no going. I am here. I turn my hand,
my mind, to whatever or fail to. Something to do.
I like it. Whatever else there is is gone.
I say it is. Changes could come again.

# TRUTH AS A FAR COUNTRY; AS A PITEOUS OGRE

There are, in many countries, cities where
thin streets are pinched between two walls
of thick exclusion, neutral and blank. Drab
gates, let in to the walls, admit us to small
flowered places, fountains, a few trees.

You know of this. You know as well those parts
of ancient stories which tell of coming, by one
means or another, and after trials, to a vast,
enchanted castle. No one, no one is there,
no one; but every place is open, as though
we were expected, or someone were. And how
the mystery adds to the pleasure we take in the food.

This is a strange world: what should we think?
The universe is very large and remote
from us. There is a kind of pleasure to think it so.
Suppose the idea of distance walls us away
as in a garden walled away from the town,
or as though a country should place a colony
(or accident should place it) so far away
the colony were perforce discrete, not
controlled by, nor controlling, anything
except itself, and thereby wholly free
to perfect itself as it would, and man free
for such image as seemed reasoned and agreeable.
A possible name for the country whose colony
we were could be Truth, wherever that is.
Who knows it, or remembers? It lies so unreachably
far distances away. Let it be.

Or, again, the pleasure of the castle stories is how
we recognize our human status here.
Thinking back, we are able to reconstruct
some parts at least of our coming, but the important thing
is to be here, to take it as it is. If it was not prepared
against our coming, no one can say we are not
adaptable. We have only to turn a hand
to find sweet pleasures, fair vistas, food, all kinds
of ingenious contrivances, and countless more
for devising. There is so much to occupy us here.
The unseen servants are marvelous.

And yet, however remote we are from truth,
or truth from us, whatever immunities
we think we have, whoever else we are, we are those
from whom the truth has no immunities.
How else should it be in the story that right from the time
we start to marvel at that fortuitous
sequence which brought us to the castle, and go about
to try its delights, we are always looking, we stop
to listen, we open doors, we go up and down
the stairs, we wake in the night? In the end we shout!
Why else is there always a piteous ogre here?
And when we see him, we know what we have to do.

# THE FEELING

One has a feeling it is all coming to an end;
no, not that. One has a feeling it is like
that war whose last battle was fought long
after the treaty was signed. The imminence
relates to a past doom. We look back
to one time, some time, something that already has
happened. Look, we are still here, but note
that nothing of moment has happened for an age, an age,
for as long as we can piece together, not
since the time it happened. Was there that time?
Once, there must have been. When will it end?

# MY HOUSE NEW-PAINTED

The splendor is not surprising; we expected it
and shine in the brightness of new paint. That the lines
should firm, though, corners sharpen, and the eaves
be reasserted, is more than we thought to ask
or look for. What is shown is a strength of the house itself
that it held in its underframing, still could hold.

We hold houses in a kind of contempt and give
them nothing, or say we do, as a way to despise
the kinds of things that houses are, all
such kinds of things, the measured entities,
that they should not be what was intended: they fail.
They burn. They fade and sag. They fall away.
We think of a time before we housed the world
or gathered things—spirits were all we saw,
spirit was real, was what there was, was all.
This was man did this, and thought to do well
when he turned away to say, on the contrary, all
the world was what we measured: houses, sums
and angles, vectors and smoothable curves. We turn,
and turn again another way to find
some way to state the world, dissatisfied
none answers.

         Still, I am pleased that my
particular house, not any way notable even,
has stood a hundred years and more, and firmed
by its shiny paint, should show the metaphor
of a material world, though it is plainly that
and nothing more—as spirit was nothing more—
could have such power now, summon it
as though from an actual world it meant to claim.
There is a world. This house can say there is.

# THE LAWN

Doubtless, it is the complex of many things
that makes it; the green for example, the color alone,
fine as that is, so intense a green, yet bland,
mild really, no, the green alone
is not enough to do it, though it is true
that yellow would be impossible, brown,
red, blue, no. It has to be green.

But it has to be more than green. There is this for one
thing amongst the many, as though there were
one, more than another, that makes the effect:
looking from slightly above it, we see that, though
by blade after blade after blade it extends a far
distance, yet against the fence and the wild field
it does end, after all. It comes to an end.

And further, in spite of small undulations, it asserts
a flat plain-ness, an assertion it carries off
with such bravura, it is as though it defied
not the curvature of the globe, only, but the curve
of space itself, went straight beyond the curve
enough to not follow, and just enough,
and hung there, overhung it. As though it did.

# THE WORLD IN TIME AND SPACE

If there is a shape to the world in terms of time
and space—our own or, by concessions to shapes
of others, received—if there is such a shape
—in part there is—note that the words we use
referring to time, as *temporary* for one
or *temporal*, admit our diffidence
toward any shape we give the world by time.

The shapes of space share less of this distrust.
we acknowledge chaotic recalcitrance
in space, its endlessness both ways, the great,
and small, and yet respect the finite shape
of bounded places, as much as to say they are true.
Some absolute of shape is stated there
which satisfies the need that makes this shape.

How strange that after all it is rarely space
but time we cling to, unwilling to let it go.

# THE BEAUTIFUL WALL, MACHU PICCHU

Greek stones look as though they'd flowed
into molds of figures, fluting, leaf forms, scrolls,
a sensed and sensible world turned stony-hard
and durable, medusaed to hold and be true,
as figure carving holds an impress pressed
on the carver's eye by a visible form whose grace
and harmony his hand lays hold and holds.
This way of handling stone is to say of the world
it is workable, and yielding and full to the hand;
and their quarrying quarried a rich world.

Looking at stones the Incas laid, abstract
austerities, unimitative stones,
so self-absorbed in their unmortared, close
accommodation, stone to different stone,
exactly interlocked, deep joined,
we see them say of the world there is nothing to say.
Who had to spend such easing care on stone
found grace inherent more as idea than in
the world, loved simple soundness in a just joint,
and the pieces together once though elsewhere apart.

## A BRIGHT DAY IN DECEMBER

So much light in what we call the dark
of the year, a flashing and glittering of light—
it quivers, it flaps in our face like slaps of wind.

Should it surprise us, having known the holes
of darkness in the longest days?

                        I have done
with promises (or say I have) of things
to come: the all-light; the all-dark;
something slow emerging; the slow (or fast)
and final decay.

                The thing we have to live
with, the last thing, is it is all
here, and was, and will be, is all there is.
Nothing is coming but what is already here
as this light, now, in the darkest time
(and nothing here that ever needed to come)
at once, too much for us and not enough.

## THE NIGHT WATCH

That limpid mirror that wakes us in the night
and watches, breathless, beside us in the bed
before we sleep again, says nothing, has
no need to say, draws commentless
its images that stun us. We never reply.
Do we dare to? How should we say? Do we even know
whether we'd rather not have seen? We know
nothing of who we are or where; this
is something, is lucid anyway; it *could*
be what we are. Is it for us to say?

# HIPPOLYTUS

I have no illusions. A certain way to ask
for trouble and be sure of no refusal, is to say
I have no illusions, and yet I say it who found
the trouble waiting at the arranged place for each
of us who met there. I know. I knew.
Which is only to say that if it had to be that,
it would have to be again: the conditions are set.
And I knew it. I knew as well as anyone knew,
besides, what inducements were offered.
                I'd been to her shrine
and felt my flesh move of its own accord
to the worship. Was this what was wanted of me? So.
It was gained. It was not I was wanting, not
what I wanted. Less, not more, and less than was promised.
And yet, I knew, knew what was promised, at least,
and failed to find it. "Give all the Gods their due,"
you say. Well, there are promises due to us
which are not kept always. "Be moderate
in all things," you say. Your things,
your moderations, as though we should all want
the same things, things that have tangible shapes.
I know what you want for yourself, and have no
objections if you want it. Leave me alone
with your moralizings. And I tell you something more:
all that hunting every day, and the poor
beasts brought home and eaten. That wasn't much;
I tell you now. It was only something to do.

## NOT MY LONELINESS, BUT OURS

The most of men are all too much myself,
my shed externals, as feces, hair, skin,
discarded clothes, useless to me and dead.
From oneness, what should we say we hadn't said
before together? Nothing to say to them,
nothing to say. As they to me, so must
I seem to them. The human loneliness -
is the endless oneness of man. Man is one;
man is alone in his world. We are the one,
even we, who whisper together now
closely, as though we were two, as children do,
knowing as much as we, and making believe,
even as we believe, that another is there.

## THERE IS IGNORANT SILENCE
## IN THE CENTER OF THINGS

What am I saying? What have I got to say?
As though I knew. But I don't. I look around
almost in a sort of despair for anything
I know. For anything. Some mislaid bit.
I must have had it somewhere, somewhere here.
Nothing. There is silence here. Were there people, once?
They must have all gone off. No, there are still
people, still a few. But the sound is off.
If we could talk, could hear each other speak,
could we piece something, could we learn and teach,
    could we know?

Hopeless. Off in the distance, busyness.
Something building or coming down. Cries.
Clamor. Fuss at the edges. What? Here,
at the center—it is the center?—only the sound
of silence, that mocking sound. Awful. Once,
before this, I stood in an actual ruin, a street
no longer a street, in a town no longer a town,
and felt the central, strong suck of it, not
understanding what I felt: the heart of things.
This nothing. This full silence. To not know.

# VIRGIN AND CHILD WITH MUSIC AND NUMBERS

Who knows better than you know,
Lady, the circumstances of this event
—meanness, the overhanging terror, and the need
for flight soon—hardly reflect the pledge
the angel gave you, the songs you exchanged in joy
with Elizabeth, your cousin? That was then
or that was for later, another time. Now—.

Still, the singing was and is. Song
whether or not we sing. The song is sung.
Are we cozened? The song we hear is like
those numbers we cannot factor whose overplus,
an indeterminate fraction, seems more than the part
we factor out. Lady, if our despair
is to be unable to factor ourselves in song
or factor the world there, what should our joy
be other than this same integer that sings
and mocks at satisfaction? We are not
fulfilled. We cannot hope to be. No,
we are held somewhere in the void of whole despair,
enraptured, and only there does the world endure.

Lady, sing to this Baby, even so.

# THE OUTER BECOMING INNER

Sometimes, I could go in anywhere, not
to see the stars, not to be as we
are always, not only under them
but in them. The outer spaces push against
us, all their vastnesses apart, they crowd
us. They become our world. I could go hide
like Adam in his garden. How
would it matter? No, we are in the stars. Not
for us ever any familiar and definite world.

# CERTAIN BEASTS, LIKE CATS

Because we do not live some life
different from the life that we do live,
sometimes I would have traded life for death
to feed my life to all that feeds on life.

Along the river, white long-legged birds
lift one foot slowly, pause to put it down,
and lift the other, down, and feed, absorbed
in certainties that never fail, though blind.

Great drifts of purple flowers hold
the roadside; patrols of purple flowers roam
through fields and climb to overtop high banks.
Purple is what color there is in the world.

Certain beasts—like cats—are sleek and quick,
their skins shimmer with light; they dream.
What force there is in fish that live their years
in the cold darks of the sea, swimming the darks.

In August once, I dozed on an unused bridge
to hang in the very world, in the teeming air.
Great world, your lives are such that we despair,
seeing the loveliness, to live our lives.

Yet men are all of these, and more than these
strong beasts, dark fish, white birds and colored flowers.

## USABLE THINGS

Only two panes out, and the birds come and go
as though the intricate place were built for them
or no, not caring, as though it were natural world
—whatever that might be.

                              Mice in the bureau drawers,
or centuries of rubbish piled in Split
in Diocletian's palace, dropped through the floors,
sifting the cellars full, Diocletian dead.

, Grace lies in the way life takes
its will with ruins, all destruction, the least
chink not stoppered, rushing in as though
it had waited for it and the best use of things
, were the second, the makeshift one.

                              Children know,
in their depredations indifferent to such intent
as we have for things: the things we make, a world.
Children are overjoyed; things are to break
or to have their pretensions broken, made usable.

# THE SUMMER AIRS

and even before that, there was such a one,
and he did thus and so.

It was much the same. It needed such deep
concentration, so many hands

he thought that if they ever let go
all this would be lost. And it was lost.

They lost it. It was a long time.
And before him also, there was one.

Who can remember the final losses?
Earth vagues the firmest bones interred.

See, here, where we are always,
in a particular, no particular time

where the summer airs flow past and over
as the congregations in air of birds.

## A POSTCARD TO SEND TO SUMER

Something you said—I found it written down—
and your picture yesterday, brought back old times.
We are here in another country now. It's hard.
(When was it ever different?) The language is odd;
we have to grope for words for what we mean.
And we hardly ever really feel at home
as though we might be happier somewhere else.
Companion, brother, (this is funny) I look
for you among the faces as if I might find
you here, or find you somewhere, and problems would then
be solved. What problems are ever solved?
Brother, the stars are almost all the same
and in good weathers—here it is summer now—
when the airs are kind, it seems the world and we
might last unchanged forever. Brother, I think
you would like it here in spite of everything.
I don't know where to send this to you. Perhaps
I'll be able to find it before the mails have closed.

# SKUNK CABBAGE

Because it is soon, it has a private and quiet
spring. Before the birds come, before
another leaf or flower, it flowers; and bees
come there and enter and leave, thick
with pollen. Foetid, even in the thin chill
of a wintry spring, it stinks of livingness,
rawness. Its color also is of skin
rubbed raw by wind, by cold, by sun,
and the flesh showing through. It is the flesh
responding to warmth, to sun, to the first spring.
It looks like tenderness, the way it curves
upward and beaks over to cover within.

# MIDSUMMER

A green world, a scene of green, deep
with light blues, the greens made deep
by those blues. One thinks how
in certain pictures, envied landscapes are seen
(through a window maybe) far behind the serene
sitter's face, the serene pose, as though
in some impossible mirror, face to back,
human serenity gazed at a green world
which gazed at this face.

                                    And see now,
here is that place, those greens
are here, deep with those blues. The air
we breathe is freshly sweet, and warm, as though
with berries. We are here. We are here.
Set this down, too, as much
as if an atrocity had happened and been seen.
The earth is beautiful beyond all change.

# THE TREE IN THE MIDDLE OF THE FIELD

The tree in the middle of the field stands round, stands tall
as though the sun hung just above forever,
and every wind were always favoring wind.

Elm branches fall with pure contemplative grace;
oak asserts without sound; a maple tree
holds a whole summer's green in one rich green.

This tree! This tree! Look, there are parts of the world
not ever wounded, within whose light, the world
is always changed with light. This tree, this tree.

# THE EXTENSIONS OF SPACE

The point must come when nothing matters more
than *who*. *What* has been heard too often; *when*
and *where* renew with shiny bangles stuff
gone dull. It is too late now for *why*.
The question is, "Who is it, is it you?"

When I came out of the house, the world, the sky,
were moving outward. There had been a big
explosion somewhere, not here, but far.
Somewhere another explosion countered. More.
The world goes whooshing. Focus is in and out.

What do we do about the tortoise? We thought
we had dispensed with that nonsense, and still
some elephant's back is wanted to hold, if not
the literal globe, our worlds, our artifacts,
our facts; and underneath, a tortoise, ground.

Only, if we go down that far,
no ground exists for facts or tortoises:
finally, we come to where there is nothing there
to underprop our worlds; logic rides high,
a balloon, and under it, we pass and go.

These are grave things, gravities,
worlds holding in suspension worlds,
and nothing under them. But also, look:
some persons bridge all across the farthest space
that we can conceive, and are solid there.

# FOR AN EARLY ITALIAN MUSICIAN

Listening now to his music, how
one wishes to have been the musician, and so
to be beautiful forever as his music is,
and he in it, who is now
only his music, which is his world.

How one always wishes for an end
— to be complete.

                    And there is also this:
that one wishes to last, that one needs to make
a world for survival, which cannot be done
simply, or soon, but by a slow
crystal on crystal accretion of a made
world, a world made to last.

One is nothing with no world.

# THE MARCHES UPSTATE

Paint-flaken, it is paint-flaken,
and the barns are tense with sagging.
The broken orchards prop themselves.

Brush-wild, it is brush-wild
and elm-tangled, and the yards
are trashed with litter of many years

as the house fronts and the business blocks
are dowdy with bare pretensions
where pity jumbles shame and show.

Road-gashed, it is road-gashed
and wire-strung. What green,
what sun, shall flesh and warm the flesh?

Loved land, unlovely, none can fit
you, for you have no shape.
Mirror in March my human face.

# THE VARIOUS SIZES OF THE WORLD

We all get used to the regular stars in time.
After the start of learning how far they are,
what distances from earth, and even more
what space they keep apart from star to star,
where centuries divide the closest star's faint light
from light beyond, the mind comes back at last
making the sky seem shallow like the earth
where, from the air, we see a city's lights
spread out across the surface crust below
in constellations we read without surprise.

The sky is a similar surface pierced with lights
until, another morning, the sensitive plate
of a telescope has fixed a light so far
we never knew, so huge that a galaxy needs
to hold it. What address ever really finds
us in the endless depths the world acquires?
The earth has mass to hold our own mass down,
and the huge sun holds earth as though
a whirled cord were taut with it. But the mind
responds to the pull of its own gravities.

The mind is shifted outward into space
beyond the sun, where the surface sky explodes
softly forever like an endless wind.
Out and back the mind, the slide of the rule.
Where shall we add the logarithm of what
to find the actual product of any hour?
What point can fix the decimal of space
that joins the least remoteness of the earth
by tiny increments to the last star?
No, here's an incongruous world, too large, too far.

# LOEW'S WORLD

Possessed of a world, however popcorn, real,
however candy-coated, the children parade
the aisles and whisper up the air, more
interested in their persons, their concerns,
the night's adventures, the sensuous amplitudes,
and less in what they have no need to find.

We, in the dark, beset by love and fear,
as by a kind of weather without terrain,
suffer the unsourced tricks of light, as when
at night in the summer, heat lightning thrusts
      from the dark
a world which was not and is gone.

                                   We
are disturbed to find so much similitude.

This unreality is one we know:
the actual is no more real than this.
I turn in my seat for the reassurance of you,
your substance which is there. Wanting a land
for our weather, a world of solid shapes, not one
the light made, we think to leave, — for where?

## ASPECTS OF THE WORLD LIKE CORAL REEFS

In the spring woods, how good it is to see
again the trees, old company,
how they have withstood the winter, their girth.

By gradual actions, how the gross earth
gathers around us and grows real, is there,
as though it were really there, and is good.

Certain stars, of stupendous size, are said
to be such and such distances away,—
oh, farther than the eyes alone would ever see.

Thus magnified, the whole evidence
of our senses is belied. For it is not
possible for miles to add miles to miles

forever, not even if expressed as the speed of light.
The fault lies partly in the idea of miles.
It is absurd to describe the world in sensible terms.

How good that even so, aspects of the world
that are real, or seem to be real, should rise like reefs
whose rough agglomerate smashes the sea.

# LA CAMA DE PIEDRA

The sun down, the ease, the speed of the night
chill make it seem in the nature of things to be cold.

The sun as intruder, suborner of earth from truth.
To be cold is the natural order of truth on the earth.

Stones that lay in the sun have held their heat,
yielding it slowly, bridging the lying suns.

But we are cold, cold, colder than stones
with hardly a hope to hold from heat to heat.

## THE BODY

Watch it. That's the body: what goes on
next door. Here, you can see it. Turn out the light;
their luminousness will show more in our dark.
What are they doing? We seldom know for sure,
but what a pleasure it is to watch. Look now!
I think he hit her, did he? We can't hear
what they say. Sometimes in summer a little. Then,
when the windows are open. But most of the time we guess.
It's like a play: he said . . .; she said . . . . Write
your own lines as you will. Or leave them blank.
Blank as they are. Or are they? You look at a back
sometimes and know it's talking. There are even times
it's almost all we want to do, to go
right over and move right in; but after all,
we live here, not there, and have, as you know,
for a long time. These people, they come and go.
But it's fascinating. There's always something new.

# BOOLEAN ALGEBRA: $X^2 = X$

Quantity is what is not. The truth
is ignorant of numbers. The universe
is one, is all; besides there is nothing. The square
of one, the square of nothing, is only one,
—or nothing. $X^2$ equals X. The truth
admits these values. What is other is not
the truth. Zero and one. An algebra
of these alone expresses everything.

But Boole was wrong; his formulas were wrong,
as Euclid was, as Newton, anyone.
Ingenious Boole. Wasn't his passion right,
that offered him to universal form
though it eluded him? One has such joy
to look at the mind of man, frail, deep
in disorder, always pushed by the falsenesses
of unreality, confined in the dark
of all we never know, yet strong with a greed
for form, the fact of which we lust toward,
believing, however often the substance is lost—
one has such joy here, it is as though
an amoeba should read to us, or snakes should sing.

# IGNORANCE AS WELL AS KNOWLEDGE HAS
# ITS PARADOXES

Mornings, we look back on sleep and see it
from another side. Like a house. We went in
through the front, and came through it, and out the back
and then looked back on it. In there,
it was different.

                        To be dead is something else again
from sleep. We don't look back on that. If it is real
at all, we must be in it and won't come out.

We are very ignorant men and know nothing about
the things that matter most to us. Remember the man
who felt so much alone, so much apart,
he said we shared a common humanity, we were all
members one of the other, each one?

# THE THINKER LEFT LOOKING OUT THE WINDOW

Looking up from his desk and from that book
he had been reading, what he had in mind
was planetary: proliferated schemes
the same for the tiniest or most immense.
The natural world, he thought, is trapped where it looks
at a mirror that reflects a mirror, a series of planes,
receding and parallel, repetitive
one to the other, and diminishing to both
distances, a circular story that tells
itself again as either a universe
or basic and particled atom. There is a lack,
he thought, of variety in structures.

                                           He
came back to the room, to what we have come to think
of as desk, as floor, as walls, and in the wall,
as window, and saw from the window the yard outside.
He thought he could use a breath of air there.
Then he considered his grossness, and thought of all
the atoms he carried with him to a door and through
that door, of how the universe
shifts with us like a shadow; or otherwise,
approaching the problem another way, he thought
of immensity so great, the parallax
between the desk and yard was negligible
so that the change in position between the two
was not to be considered as something gained.

No, there was only this, and what was there for it?

# THE ARIA

He lets us into a room which must
be any room in an ordinary
house on a street where buses, perhaps,
go past us, or once we arrived just
too late to watch a parade. This
is a city, anyway, where
we always seem to be at the wrong
season; the weather is bad, and our friends
are somewhere else. Here in the room
though, there is a fragrance we had all
but forgotten from somewhere, and all around
us, a great ingathering of lovely things
from such long distances of time
and space, we marvel to see again,
and for once together, what we have failed
before to connect. Or so it seems.
Does it matter that on a second look
the room is empty, or if not that,
that the things that are gathered here are things
we never saw before? No.
With what sweet eloquence
these objects speak and ask no reply;
for listen, it is we, ourselves, who sing.

# HOW INDETERMINACY DETERMINES US

We are so little discernible as such
in so much nothing, it is our privacy
sometimes that startles us: the world is ours;
it is only ours; others that move there,
or seem to, are elsewhere, are in another world,
their world; only, we see from time to time
—shattered, as though we were nothing, or not
stable—sometimes we see what they see,
no world we know. Theirs. Strange. As though
by a momentary shift of little bits
of charges, copper were carbon and felt the weight
and valences of carbon in a changed field
of inertias and reactions, and then were copper again
in a cupreous world. We are left to wonder at
and ponder our privacy and ponder this:
we are two unknowns in a single equation, we
and our world, functions one of the other. Sight
is inward and sees itself, hearing, touch,
are inward. What do we know of an outer world?

# HOW WE DIFFER FROM THE EARTH

Early autumn. Watching the light run out.
As though by the sea. An estuary. The light
runs like a tide running. Swiftly. Flat.
How the flat light rushes to be gone,
sucked by the gravitation of the low sun.
The wash of light coming and going, the year,
the many weathers that return, travel in flat
circles. There were long centuries
before the earth was round. The earth-flats
are there, still, to be seen, as one sees,
still, of the weather, it is there, and runs in flat
circles, whereas we—no! What
have earth or the weather, in the end, to do
with us, who, in a world of our own, despite
them, or even unaware, live for a time all
bulks and prominences, wide and high!

## TENOCHTITLAN

I did not go to Coatlicue today,
to her of the writhing skirt of serpents, skulls
suspended at her neck, clawed Mother of the Gods.

Not that it mattered: if we have learned at all,
we have learned not to deny the terrible ones
their due; they have it; we are theirs to keep.

But we also learn — not knowing is it fear
or defiance teaching us — not to think
of everything always, sometimes not to think.

Xilonen, Goddess of the Young Corn, of green
and growing, grant us the solace of sweet ears
soft in the mouth; accept our truant love.

We drink to you, Xilonen, we are drunk
with deep pleasures and a deep need, drunk
with gentleness and the pleasure of gentle needs.

# THE NATURE OF THE UNIVERSE

Was it Scheherazade who told, among
other tales, of a nightmare hole, a dark
cave of horror, a passageway where beasts
we could not see struck at us,
something smothered the face with softness, there
was slime on the hands, and caution quieted
that pressure that pushed in the throat like either a call
or a full revulsion, lest, rather than aid,
a call bring further horror from the same ones
we hoped might aid us, and we were afraid of them?

The passage led to a place where jewels shone
of their own light and this light everywhere
was both the water and the music of that place.

If not Scheherazade, no matter. We know
these places and have been to them.

If there is One, and all we know is One,
and there is no other, nothing, as nightly, the far
glitter of distant stars proclaims it, we
are the inner mirror of those stars, who find
only an ecstasy to outfeel
horror, and be blind to that sight that:
we are nowhere, there is no other place,
and nothing to turn to, in solitude.

## NOT SATELLITE

Yes, like the sun for warmth for splendor of light;
you are all that. I think always such light
here or wherever and even behind, beyond,
the farthest reach of time, of space, the big
stars, those suns, forever burning. No space
without stars: this magnificence is true.
No escape. Where the eyes do not go or need to go
still stars. No escape. I acknowledge and am glad:
not satellite in such a world!

# A BLACK CLAY FISH FROM OAXACA

First though, look at this mask. It came from the same
city, or near there. Dug from a grave.
The original was gold as this would seem
to be, but isn't. This is silver gilt.
But feel the weight of it and see how rich
the decorations are: the ear plugs,
the nose-pendant, the fringe around the head.
It is a mask of Spring. The heaviness
of the huge, thick-lidded eyes is brought about
by what hangs over them: this represents
a sheet of human skin. The power of the thing
is in that inward smoldering, all overlaid.
Here is the fine fish. Isn't he fat!
Such sleek blackness; and happy, they say, as a trout.

# THE NATURE OF MUSICAL FORM

It is hard to believe of the world that there should be
music in it: these certainties against
the all-uncertain, this ordered fairness beneath
the tonelessness, the confusion of random noise.

It is tempting to say of the incomprehensible,
the formlessness, there is only order as we
so order and ordering, make it so; or this,
there is natural order which music apprehends

which apprehension justifies the world;
or even this, these forms are false, not true,
and music irrelevant at least, the world
is stated somewhere else, not there. But no.

How is it? There is a fairness of person too,
which is not a truth of persons or even, we learn,
a truth of that person, particularly.
It is only fairness stating only itself:

as though we could say of music only, it is.

## THAT LITTLE VARIANCE:
## EXTENSIONS OF A THEME FROM JOSEPH CONRAD

"Gentlemen," he said, "we remember a time
and remember with sadness now, a time when life
seemed still ahead of us; we worked toward
it, and while anticipated, it was gone.
Gentlemen—," he said. They nodded assent.

They must have worked the wrong way round.
Isn't it easy to see that now?
Isn't it easy to say that now?
No, it is nothing said. Whatever way
would be the wrong way. There is no right.

It is too little to say that time is short. If it stretched
wherever, no matter. It extends wherever. Add on,
add on. The units of time—hours, days,
dismay us by their extension. Time which divides
anywhere we divide it, goes on.

These long divisions mean nothing in human terms.
Divide or multiply, add on, subtract,
and any piece is all simply in not
being all, in incompleteness. Time which is gone
while still anticipated is incomplete.

We are less creatures than other creatures are.
Plants, particularly, are specific within
their variety. They come as they are and fruit
in their time. Their directions are adequate and complete.
And with the animals, it is likewise true:

young lions are soon leonine,
amphibians and insects trace
in time quite diverse stages, unhesitant.
Their fixed identity survives the most
successful disguises and comes true. They are as they are.


Beauty varies without increase and the same
is true of terror. Nothing we ever do
is final. By this are we deprived of time
unless that little variance were time.
But we desire it not to be. We want

a time that completes itself, that begins and ends,
that makes an end, that alters for once and all
the little variance and holds it still,
even if the end it makes is a final end:
that want includes a will to destroy ourselves.

They have their times and die. They die in time.
Aye, gentlemen, who are we? The natural man
is something less than man, is hardly man.
He has his time. What time have we whose time
while still anticipated yet is gone?

Our now is a now unrealized. We are less
creatures than other creatures are. We have
no time. Wishing to be, we find we don't
know how. What shall we be? And yet we are,
somehow we are. Our now is a long now.

We recognize our fellow bones in the ground.
Dug things talk to us in languages
we know; and we, uncertain how to call
our name, our place, are eased and fortified
to say, not "here we were", but "here we are".

Man has a time different from other time,
time unfulfilled, unrealized, gone
while still anticipated. This is the kind
it is but not its length. Nobody knows
its length, if it has length. Gentlemen —

# GREEN AS A VERITY

Do you see the light on those green trees?
Green is real in an intensity of green.

Deciduousness is nothing, as evergreen
is nothing either. These are not the point.

Certain situations lack all green,
or it is there in all variety.

But this is not the point. Exactly not.
Who denies it: we are not told

anything we can believe in, and we live
in a hardly credible world? What is not

hidden from us? Our reasonings confuse
us and obscure what little we think to see of the world.

It is that kind of a place; but even so,
some things cannot stay hidden, are obvious.

We stumble on them and wonder how or why
we missed it before, that, for instance, green

is a verity, not to be reckoned without
in its absence even, in places where it is not,

and there are such places and such times.
The idea of green. That there are verities.

## THE OUTCRY

What I want to do is shout. Happiness? No.
Outrage? No. What I want to do is shout
because we were all wrong, because the point
was not the point, because the world, or what
we took for the world, is breaking, breaking. We were wrong
and are not right. Break! Break! We are here!
What I want to do is shout! Break! Shout!

Other New Directions — San Francisco Review Books:

James B. Hall, *Us He Devours*. Short stories.

George Oppen, *The Materials*. Poems.

Charles Reznikoff, *By the Waters of Manhattan*. Poems.

*San Francisco Review Annual No. 1*. Anthology of new prose and poetry.

Curtis Zahn, *American Contemporary*. Short stories.